HOW TO LISTEN TO GOD

9 CHANNELS YOU MUST USE TO UNDERSTAND GOD'S ANSWER TO YOUR PRAYER

VITALIS ESSALA

Copyright © 2024 Vitalis Essala.

All rights reserved. No part of this book may be reproduced, stored, or transmitted by any means—whether auditory, graphic, mechanical, or electronic—without written permission of both publisher and author, except in the case of brief excerpts used in critical articles and reviews. Unauthorized reproduction of any part of this work is illegal and is punishable by law.

ISBN: 979-8-89419-149-2 (sc)
ISBN: 979-8-89419-150-8 (hc)
ISBN: 979-8-89419-151-5 (e)

Because of the dynamic nature of the Internet, any web addresses or links contained in this book may have changed since publication and may no longer be valid. The views expressed in this work are solely those of the author and do not necessarily reflect the views of the publisher, and the publisher hereby disclaims any responsibility for them.

One Galleria Blvd., Suite 1900, Metairie, LA 70001
(504) 702-6708

Dedication

*To Daniella Essala and Samuella Essala,
my dear daughters.*

Contents

INTRODUCTION 1

CHAPTER 1: READ THE WORD OF GOD 5

To Stay Tuned in God's Communication System, the Bible Is the Easiest Channel 7

Not Every Need Is Spelled Out in the Bible 10

Read: you Will Hear God 11

CHAPTER 2: TALK TO GOD AND WAIT 13

Is God anyone to you? 14

CHAPTER 3: LISTEN TO THE MESSAGES PREACHED TO YOU 17

God Still Speaks Through his Preachers 18

God Is Not Boring 19

CHAPTER 4: USE FLEECES AND ASK FOR SIGNS 21

CHAPTER 5: READ THE SIGNS AND WATCH THE CIRCUMSTANCES 25

Let us Digress 26
Do Not Be Deceived 27
Listen 28

CHAPTER 6: UNDERSTAND DREAMS AND VISIONS 29

It Is a Gift of God to Interpret Dreams 31
God Enables those that Are Obedient 32

CHAPTER 7: LISTEN TO YOUR HEART 35

God Instructs our Heart 36
I Can Hear God Speak 37

CHAPTER 8: ASK FOR ADVICE 39

CHAPTER 9: GOD SPEAKS AUDIBLY 43

CONCLUSION 47

Read God's Word 48
Talk to God Always 49
Listen to the Preached Message 49
Use Fleeces 50
Watch the Signs 51
Pay Attention to your Dreams 51
Listen to your Heart 52

Seek Advice 53
Listen to the Audible Voice of God 54

ABOUT THE AUTHOR 55

OTHER PRODUCTS FROM THIS AUTHOR 57
Books 57
Audio CDs and Downloadables 58
Online Courses 58

CONTACT THE AUTHOR 59

Introduction

My friend,

Our life is full of frustrations and despair even when we spend time studying the Word of God and praying. We do not always understand what is going on and how to get God to intervene in our life. It can be hard to believe that God hears us when we pray. How does God hear us if He cannot answer us? But the Bible does not lie.

> *"Now this is the confidence that we have in Him, that if we ask anything according to His will, He hears us." (1 John 5:14)*

Besides the fact that the Bible affirms that if we pray God hears us, there is another confusing statement in this passage. What is the will of God?

My friend, it is not in our best interest to spend time right now cogitating on what the will of God is and how to pray according to His will. As important as it can be, we are not going to focus on that topic right now. Let's focus on the first part of 1 John 5:14.

Now this is the confidence that we have in Him. If there is anyone who will never fail us, that is God. So, how is it that our confidence is betrayed almost all the time? Okay, before we get any further with these troubling questions, let's cut it short that God is faithful, and He never does betray anyone. He always hears us. He always answers us from the first moment we open our mouth to pray. How do I know this? He said it and we see it throughout the Bible.

One of the most vivid examples is Daniel spending three weeks to pray.

"But the prince of the kingdom of Persia withstood me twenty-one days; and behold, Michael, one of the chief princes, came to help me, for I had been left alone there with the kings of Persia." (Daniel 10:13)

Here is Daniel, a perfect man, praying and waiting. The first day he had humbled himself to pray, God sent Gabriel, the angel, to answer his prayer. But an archangel represented here as "the prince of the kingdom of Persia" blocked him for three weeks. Michael, another archangel, an angel higher in rank than Gabriel, came to lend a hand to Gabriel.

Now, you will tell me that not everyone is as perfect as Daniel. But "God [b]shows personal favoritism to no man." (Galatians 2:6) Everyone has the same access to God. If you have access to God, He will answer you the same way He would answer anyone else. That does not mean that He is always going to give us what we ask. It just means that God will send us an answer. An answer can be "Yes," "No," or "Wait." God always hears and answers us. If we do not see anything happening, it means that we do not pay attention.

All the answers do not come the way it came to Daniel. In Daniel's case, God chose to send an answer through the mouth of an angel. But this is not the only way He responds to our prayer and that is where we are mistaken. There are multiple other ways God answers us. We must be aware of those other ways and be open to them. The following ways will help you decode God's answer to you more efficiently.

CHAPTER 1

Read The Word Of God

The Bible is almost the perfect way God uses to talk to us. Almost because I have no pretention to decide which way is the best that God uses to communicate with us. But since other ways are either difficult to understand or seldom happen, it is wise to say that the Bible is the best and most likely channel God uses to communicate His will to us.

If you want to know what God thinks of humankind, what He thinks of this world, and what is going to happen to the world, the Bible has the best answer. God put His will in there to educate, reprove, and encourage us.

> *"All Scripture is given by inspiration of God, and is profitable for doctrine, for reproof, for correction, for instruction in righteousness." (2 Timothy 3:16)*

God spelled out His will: what He wants us to know and do every day is in the word. There is no better way to listen to God than to read in His word. Before you pray, read the word of God. It will give you knowledge on how to pray and what to ask for. After you pray, read the Bible again and listen to what it's going to tell you. If you make this a habit of yours, you will be amazed on how familiar you will become with the will of God. You will grow in faith, in love for God, and in grace because you think like God.

To Stay Tuned in God's Communication System, the Bible Is the Easiest Channel

It is easy to listen to God through His word. Think about this: If you asked 100 people who know God what their favorite Bible verse is, they will each give you one. And sometimes people will give you the verses you wouldn't think would be a favorite to anyone. Why do you think everyone has a favorite Bible verse? I am going to give you my answer shortly, but let's address another question that might be ruminating in your mind.

If I pray for a car, what does that have to do with the Bible? How is the Bible going to help me hear God's voice concerning a new car that I want?

Indeed, the Bible has everything to do with your want or need for a new car. There is no need in human life that God did not think of when He put His will in the form of a book we call the Bible. No wonder some of us find solace in a verse that would make no sense to others in similar situations. The Bible has everything to do with the need you have for a car. This is how we know it.

> *Matthew 6:8. "Be not ye therefore like unto them: for your Father knoweth what things ye have need of, before ye ask him."*

If God knows our need before we ask, He also has the provision before we ask. But how could we have this assurance if we don't know His word? Now let's read random verses to see how God can speak to us and address our concern for any need we might bring to Him.

> "So the children of Israel went into the midst of the sea on the dry ground, and the waters were a wall to them on their right hand and on their left." (Exodus 14:22)

If you know this verse, you know that if God can divide a sea in half, He is able to do anything, including the car you are asking for. That knowledge will grow your faith and trust. You will pray with assurance, and work toward getting your car with much ease.

> "And my God shall supply all your need according to His riches in glory by Christ Jesus." (Philippians 4:19)

If you know this verse, you will understand that God supplies all needs. All we must do is to ask in the name of Jesus. How difficult is it to do that? Not difficult at all.

> "And whatever things you ask in prayer, believing, you will receive." (Matthew 21:22)

If you know this verse, you know that your car is also included in this promise. Whatever is everything that is necessary and does not go against morality and law. Your asking for a car is a necessity. Therefore, it is included in the whatever of Matthew 21.

> "Who provides food for the raven, When its young ones cry to God, And wander about for lack of food?" (Job 38:41)

If you know this verse, you know that you are more valuable than the raven. Therefore, God will provide for you. No questions asked. Yes, it is easy to hear God through His word.

Not Every Need Is Spelled Out in the Bible

God has our best interest in mind. He knows that we must commute daily. Therefore, He wants us to get that car. While you may not see written in the Bible that if you need a car, this is the verse you should read, you can still listen to God through His word.

My favorite verse in the Bible is Zacchariah 4:6. So he answered and said to me: "This is the word of the Lord to Zerubbabel: '**Not by might nor by power, but by My Spirit', Says the Lord of hosts**."

The core of the verse for me is the bolded part. Even though the Bible does not talk about a car in a direct manner, every time I would pray for a car, I would hear God say to me that I should not count on the savings in my account or be desperate because of the money I don't have, for it is not by might nor by power, but by the Spirit of God that I will get a car. You, likewise, every time you pray, must use your favorite verse and recite it back to God. When you want to build your faith and be confident that God is going to answer you, recite your favorite verse.

Read: you Will Hear God

This technique of the favorite verse is when you have nothing else. But I can promise you that if you familiarize yourself with the word of God, you will be amazed to see how God talks to you clearly through some passages in the Bible. Read the Bible more frequently than usual. You will hear God speak to you.

CHAPTER 2

Talk To God And Wait

There is a taboo around prayer that the devil created to stop us from yielding the results God intended for our lives. Don't fall prey to that taboo. It is easy to talk to God. Figure having a best friend. Is it difficult or easy to talk to your best friend? If it's easy, then it is easier to talk to God.

God is the best friends of ours among the best friends we have. He is the most loving Father we can dream of. For that reason, we must talk to Him in any language and in our terms. We don't need any formal language or master any commanding protocol. If you want to talk to God right now, just open your mouth and start talking to Him. No one should impose on you what to say or how to say it when you talk to God. Even though I teach people how to pray, that has nothing to do with teaching a certain binding list of things to memorize. If you want to talk to God, do it in a way that feels comfortable to you.

Is God anyone to you?

The first question to ask yourself is, "Who is God to me?" If God is a friend, talk to Him as to a friend. If God is a father to you, talk to Him as to a loving father. If you have a traumatizing earthly father, I want to assure you, God is a better father. Talk to Him as to the person you wish your father was.

The second question to ask is, "How is our relationship?" Just because you think God is your friend or father or whomever does not mean that you entertain the same relationship with Him. God is your friend, for sure. But are you His friend? Do you treat Him as a friend or just as someone who comes to you with gifts and goodies?

I am not saying this to make you uncomfortable or to say that God holds a grudge. It is for your own comfort. It is to urge you to examine yourself when you come to God.

When you come to God, you have something (or must have something) in mind. You want Him to hear you. Fortunately, He wants to hear you. You want to hear from Him also. Once again, He wants you to hear Him. He wants to bless you with His word, and He wants to guide you in your journey. He likes this communication.

Talking to God is a communication. There is no communication that is one-sided. If you write to someone all the time without hearing back from them, you can't say that you are in communication with that person. In a communication, you act and the interlocuter responds. This means that when you talk to God, you must listen to Him also. He will talk back.

God speaks in various ways. He may use your mind to tell you something or your heart to make you have a certain sentiment or feeling. Usually, the feelings or thoughts that you have during prayer about your problem or some other issues of interest come from God. But there is a caution to that statement. You need to tell these thoughts apart whether they are God's, the enemy's, or yours.

There is no better way to say it. But keep in mind that when you talk to God, He will hear you and talk back to you. Pray to Him to help you know how to listen to Him and how to know when it is Him who is talking. Sometimes, God will answer the prayer you made this morning in the message you will hear today. Therefore, pay attention to every message you hear.

CHAPTER 3

Listen To The Messages Preached To You

In times past, when someone wanted to hear from God, he came to the seer. The seer is what we call a prophet today. Prophets have the gift of the ministry of standing between God and the people. Even though God talks equally to everyone, He invests a special ability on some individuals to decode God's message more skillfully than others.

God Still Speaks Through his Preachers

Nowadays, there is a lot of noise about preachers. People listen less and less to preachers. Part of this is because preachers have proven themselves unworthy because the unprofessional behavior they project and the impious messages they profess from the pulpit. But another part is the parishioners themselves choosing to shun the voice of God. All of it is the work of the devil.

The art of preaching is so essential to Christian growth that the first apostles linked it together with prayer when conflicts arose among brethren in the first church. *"But we will give ourselves continually to prayer and to the ministry of the word."* (Acts 6:4)

These two ministries (prayer and the preaching of the word) are the core ministries of church leaders. Prayer is talking to God, lifting the people to God, and the preaching of the word is explaining the will of God to the community.

If you want to hear the voice of God, one best medium is the preaching of the word. In fact, every time you hear someone preach, take it seriously. God always speaks in that instance. Whether it is a child or an experienced preacher, God will always have something to say to His people. If you listen to the message to hear God, you will hear Him even when the message is being preached by the most unqualified person.

God Is Not Boring

It is unfortunate that we all make this mistake. We find some sermons to be boring. But the Lord is not boring. If we find a sermon to be boring, it is a mistake. Maybe the preacher didn't prepare well, but the sermon is not to be boring.

The sermon is one of the official ways God teaches His will to His children. A sermon is God's lecture to His students. When we go to church, we go to the school of Zion. We learn the manners and heavenly etiquettes. Each person who wants to graduate someday must listen carefully to God through the sermon.

What do you do when your instructor is not engaging? Very rarely do you drop the course. We should not disconnect from listening to a sermon because it is not going the way we thought it would. We must learn to learn from different perspectives.

Before the sermon begins, or an exhortation, or just a word of advice, prepare your heart to listen to God. In fact, it is early in the morning that you prepare your heart to listen to God that day. If you are going to church, ask the Holy Spirit to open your heart to listen to God. If it is a pop message, then ask God to help you listen emphatically and take action. If you do, you will learn the best way to listen to God through sermons and preached messages even when a message is not too palatable. If you truly want to hear God's voice, you will hear Him speak to you. If not by sermons, He can speak to you by fleeces. Gideon used fleeces to decipher God's will. You can do the same for your life.

CHAPTER 4

Use Fleeces And Ask For Signs

"So Gideon said to God, 'If You will save Israel by my hand as You have said—look, I shall put a fleece of wool on the threshing floor; if there is dew on the fleece only, and it is dry on all the ground, then I shall know that You will save Israel by my hand, as You have said.'" And it was so. When he rose early the next morning and squeezed the fleece together, he wrung the dew out of the fleece, a bowlful of water. Then Gideon said to God, 'Do not be angry with me, but let me speak just once more: Let me test, I pray, just once more with the fleece; let it now *be dry only on the fleece, but on all the ground let there be dew.' And God did so that night. It was dry on the fleece only, but there was dew on all the ground." (Judges 6:36-40)*

It is okay to doubt our perception of God's answer. It is ideal to accept God's answer when it comes. But if we are not sure, we can double check with God by using a fleece. Only, a fleece in your context does not have to be of wool. It can be a sign or an occurrence. You can ask God to make something happen for you to know this is what He is telling you to do.

If you remember the story I told in my program, **The 5 Models of Prayer,** of a brother who prayed for a wife, you know this is a fleece. The brother went early to church and asked God to send his wife. The first unmarried sister that would show up at church would be his wife. Some people have asked for the rain. Anyone can use the fleece. I have used the fleece before. But if you use the fleece, unless someone else is praying with you for the same purpose, don't share it until the thing is known.

If you want to use this technique to listen to God, I advise you to ask for a clear sign. If you ask God to make the temperature of the entire week to be mild, that is not clear. Even though God knows what you mean by mild in your own terms, the risk is that you might forget what you meant by mild then. If you want to use the temperature, which I don't think is clear, maybe ask that the weather forecast be totally changed tomorrow.

If the prediction is 80% chance of rain with thunderstorms tomorrow, ask that there be no rain at all and that the day be sunny, with clear skies, and that the weather person of X channel exclaim on the TV that they don't know what just happened. These are extensive specifications you can't miss. But again, God is sovereign. Asking for something like this might not be done because it will affect other climatic phenomena, and God is not ready to upset the entire creation to satisfy your request.

The problem with the fleece is that people fear to ask for too difficult signs as if God was limited by the scope of actions. If you feel that the sign you are about to ask for is too unlikely to happen, then don't ask for it. Either that will not happen because God is not going to change the entire train of action in nature to satisfy your request or you don't have enough faith in that sign. Use a different fleece and read the signs perfectly.

CHAPTER 5

Read The Signs And Watch The Circumstances

"Of the sons of Issachar who had understanding of the times, to know what Israel ought to do, their chiefs were two hundred; and all their brethren were at their command" (1 Chronicles 12:32)

David is now king. Army officials are pouring in from all sides to ally with him. Among them, these sons of Issachar came. They were especially gifted because they knew how to read the times and the circumstances. They wouldn't just engage in anything because the crowd was doing it. They did something because they felt the time was right for it.

One way God speaks to us is by these signs. Sometimes, you will just feel that this is the right time to do this or that. Sometimes, someone will say something that will draw your attention. Sometimes, something will just happen that will ring the bell.

Let us Digress

Politicians know how to read the signs. Those that have good strategists act in specific times. They feed the media with what they want. They speak up when the time is appropriate. All these strategies are what gets them elected.

The signs do not only show themselves in politics. When you pray for something, pray with open eyes, pray with your feet, and pray with your feelings. God might stir up something that will tell you, "This is it; go ahead!"

Do Not Be Deceived

The devil also tricks people in many ways. He has the knowledge of time too. When he hears you pray for something, he could cause an event to happen that will distract you. This is scary. The good news is God is always up close to lead you out of the trap. To follow God's guidance, do not just jump into the first circumstance. If you do, you will increase your likelihood of erring.

Joshua walked with God from his youth through his service to Moses, the servant of God, until the day he made a decision without consulting with God. In Joshua 9, you read the story of the Gibeonites who deceived Joshua by telling him that they came from a far country to make a covenant with him. Joshua did not pray to check this out, and he was deceived.

Do not let the distraction of the devil deceive you. When you get the feeling that this is the right time to do X or Y, pray again and ask God if this is the package He sent to your direction. If you are still not clear, ask someone you trust and who trusts God. If you are a man, listen to your wife's gut feeling.

Listen

I once had a job. It did not pay a lot, but it was consistent. Then I had another offer. A better offer. My wife didn't feel it was the right move, but I convinced myself that she was wrong. Guess what? I lost that would-be better offer in such a painful way that left me out of work for a long time. Don't just take my word for it. Ask married men who have been married for decades. Read the signs with your feelings, your loved ones' feelings, and God's approval. Do not just go because this fits your dreams and visions.

CHAPTER 6

Understand Dreams And Visions

"'And it shall come to pass in the last days, says God, That I will pour out of My Spirit on all flesh; Your sons and your daughters shall prophesy, Your young men shall see visions, Your old men shall dream dreams.'" (Acts 2:17)

God is not giving us these prophecies, visions, and dreams to decorate our nights. He is doing it to equip us, talk to us, and enable us for His mission for us. Everything we do must align with God's mission for us. Our mission is to go to the world and make disciples of all the nations. In the meantime, we must provide for ourselves and our families. We must go to the hospital. We must get education and follow a career. This is where we interact with God concerning these secondary tasks.

God will also use dreams, prophecies, and visions to teach us about our daily lives regarding our secondary tasks of living. Therefore, we must ask God to help us understand the meaning of the dreams He gives us. Dreams here are the literal dreams we have when we sleep. They are also the desires we nurture in our mind and goals we set. God will give us dreams and visions to decode and succeed in our respective situations.

Joseph and Daniel are not just known for their good stewardship or loyalty to their pagan kings. They set themselves apart by the gift of interpreting dreams. Those are gifts given by God. God is not a man to change. If He gave that gift to the people that lived before us; He also gives the same gift to our contemporaneous brethren.

One of the reasons we do not enjoy our dreams is that we do not pay that much attention to dreams anymore. But discarding an entire medium of communication with God that way is making a costly mistake, mostly because we know that God said He would use this medium more frequently in the last days. Who is here who doubts that we are living in the last days?

It Is a Gift of God to Interpret Dreams

We probably know someone or have heard of someone who's dreams usually mean something is going to happen. What do parents do when their child has the ability to remember his or her dreams and clearly predict the future? They repress this ability in the child because it is similar to witchcraft. But the understanding of the dream is a gift. Do you know why only Daniel was known to be able to interpret dreams? Maybe because he was the only one who had ever dared asking God to show him the dreams and their interpretations.

God spoke to prophets in dreams. (Numbers 12:6) We have a Bible full of those words that came in dreams. We base our entire faith on those dreams. What had changed? God, us, dreams? We need to come back to the basics.

God Enables those that Are Obedient

Have you ever asked God to tell you the interpretation of your dream? Singers dream some of their best songs. People make inventions from what they saw in the dream. Moses saw a vision of the tabernacle. It wasn't a picture presented to him in his fleshly eyes. But no one questions that. If you were to go to church nowadays and utter that you saw a vision, people would look at you as at a heretic and an apostate. But by the grace of God, I am telling you that God speaks through dreams also. If you dream a dream, ask God to help you remember it and interpret it. Listen to your heart and not so much to what people will think.

CHAPTER 7

Listen To Your Heart

Your heart is valuable to God. He put the heart in us as a transponder through which He communicates with us. Heaven can track us through our heart. Depending on how our heart is (pure or filthy) the signal becomes vibrant in heaven or dim. This is why God tells us to keep our heart with all diligence, "for out of it spring the issues of life." (Proverbs 4:23).

Life for God is not just natural life. It is also spiritual life. We love with our heart, including God. We do not love God with our brain or else it is not true love. If our heart is pure and loves God without hindrance, our path to heaven is paved in crimson. The blood of Jesus will keep it navigable.

God Instructs our Heart

God speaks to us through our heart. Sometimes our head will think this sounds right, but our heart will not stop cricking in disapproval. So, for you to gauge God's green light for something, check with your heart. Is your heart at peace with this decision? If you are accustomed to keeping your heart with all diligence, it will be a trusted checkpoint to guide you in God's ways. But if your heart is full of anger, impurity, pride, or the cares of this world, it will not lead you well.

You may still be wondering how we do hear God's voice talking to our heart. If that's the case, that is a good concern to have. Let's not make this too difficult than it is. Have you ever had this happen to you? A random thought just crosses your mind and you just brush it off as just a thought. A few minutes down the road you get into an argument or accident, or you just miss an opportunity that does not come around every day. If you think this is your sixth sense, you're right! But God uses our sixth sense to communicate to our heart.

I Can Hear God Speak

Let me tell you how I usually hear God speak. Most of the time, when I pray for something, I feel as someone just stopped me and started talking to me. I do not hear an audible voice. But when I stop, someone is talking to me clearly about what is going to happen or what I should do. Sometimes this voice's instruction has nothing to do with what I'm praying for, and when it does respond to the subject of my prayer, sometimes it goes to the opposite direction of the thought I initially had. And every time I follow the instruction or guidance I receive through this channel, the result is positive.

God speaks to our heart. We must listen to Him and prepare our heart to receive His communication. If we don't listen to this channel, we will miss one of the best channels the Most-High uses to teach His people. At times, it will happen that no matter what we do, we won't just know what God's guidance is concerning one aspect of our life. In that case, we must seek advice.

CHAPTER 8

Ask For Advice

I suppose you already know that I'm going to use the best Bible verse there is when it comes to advice or counsel. Proverbs 15:22 says "Without counsel, plans go awry, But in the multitude of counselors they are established." The Bible repeats here what it says in Proverbs 11:14. This is not an all-inclusive truth. We do not always need many counselors to act on our life. But before you crucify me that I am criticizing the Bible, let's agree that the idea of this Bible verse is that knowledge is not a one-man-show business: knowledge is obtained in a collegial association. With that being said, the necessity of seeking advice comes when there is no clear picture of what God wants us to do.

You are not an immature Christian if you seek advice. In fact, maturity is shown when we seek advice from others because we know in part. God created us in a society to learn and grow together. The people that are around us are here to hold us high when we need them. The rule of thumb would be to ask for advice from our spiritual leaders, parents, or people of experience. That does not mean that we cannot seek advice from younger persons.

The tip to keep in mind is to have someone (a prayer partner, a God-fearing friend, or spiritual leader) with whom you have a good relationship. That person will be ideal to turn to for advice. But everything you do, do it in prayer. Even when someone is your best friend, you should still bring them to God's attention before you talk to them. If God wants them to find you the right help, then thank Him.

Before you go and ask someone for advice, you must know their reputation. Who are they? How is their walk with the Lord? Just because they hold a certain position is not a go-go. Even when you don't know them on a personal level, you must find out about them. Don't we do that with anyone we want to hire? We check their resume and reference. We vet them in a way. When it comes to knowing God's plan for your life, be careful who you ask for advice from.

Does it mean that we should only ask angels for advice? No. Humans are fallible. No one will be impeccable. Yet we should still work with them regardless of their flaws. Only, we should cover a certain number of prerequisites. If someone has failed at something you are working on, has learned something, and has moved on, that could be a good person to seek advice from: they have been here before. So, have a few criteria your advisor should meet before you hire them, so to speak. Remember that we are all humans. You will not find a perfect person, but make sure you go to someone who will help you hear God's voice.

CHAPTER 9

God Speaks Audibly

There are not many passages in the Bible where God speaks to people audibly. Moses was just one of those fortunate human beings God chose to communicate with mouth to mouth. In fact, he is the only prophet God spoke to in that manner. When Aaron and Miriam spoke against Moses in the wilderness, God set the tone by reminding them how different Moses was.

"Hear now My words: If there is a prophet among you, I, the Lord, make Myself known to him in a

> *vision; I speak to him in a dream. Not so with My servant Moses; He is faithful in all My house. I speak with him face to face, Even plainly, and not in dark sayings; And he sees the form of the Lord. Why then were you not afraid To speak against My servant Moses?" (Numbers 12:6-8)*

Samuel heard someone call him when he was a child in the temple. He thought it was Eli, the high priest, who called him. Paul heard a voice from heaven as he went to Damascus.

> *"Now it happened, as I journeyed and came near Damascus at about noon, suddenly a great light from heaven shone around me. And I fell to the ground and heard a voice saying to me, 'Saul, Saul, why are you persecuting Me?' So I answered, 'Who are You, Lord?' And He said to me, 'I am Jesus of Nazareth, whom you are persecuting.'" (Acts 22:6-8)*

As He predicted His death on the cross, the crowd that stood by heard "an angel" speaking to Jesus from heaven. "Therefore the people who stood by and heard it said that it had thundered. Others said, 'An angel has spoken to Him.'" (John 12:29)

Several people have said to have heard God's voice. I believe this is possible. It is usually in trying times that God comes to reassure His servants that He is standing by them. But this is not an ongoing occurrence. Even when that happens, the conversation is very brief. So, it is unlikely that you will hear God's voice audibly very often. But if God speaks to you audibly, listen to Him.

Conclusion

My friend,

We have now come to the end of this program. Thank you for following along with me. The Lord be with you. Listen to Him. He will speak to you. You discovered nine ways to check God's answers today. Use all of them. When it comes to listening to God, we cannot choose what we like best. We use all the channels our Father uses. Therefore, study this material several times to see if you are not leaving one channel out of use. You will hear God more often, and why not always, if you check with Him on every channel He gave us.

Read God's Word

Let no day go by without you reading the word of God. It is one thing to listen to audio Bibles. Faith comes by hearing the word of God. But it is another thing to read the word. If you know how to read and you are not confined away from the Bible, I admonish you, read at least one verse a day. You will hear God speak to you. His voice through the Bible will grow clearer and clearer than you ever imagined. This following recommendation is not an option: read the entire Bible from Genesis 1:1 to Revelations 22:21, once per year. We are children of the Kingdom. What else could we possibly have which would be that much important to us!

When diplomats represent their country in another land, they are connected to their home country. Every communication that comes from the president or any other type of leader is in the country is taken seriously. Every personnel of the consulate will read it and follow it. We are ambassadors in this world. Our president, the Lord has sent us a communication. We must take it seriously.

Talk to God Always

God loves us. He wants to commune with us. He is not overwhelmed. So, there is never a bad time to go to our Heavenly Father. He enjoys seeing us playing on the porch of His house. He loves seeing us bump into His knees while looking straight in His eyes. He loves hearing our soft voice calling Him, "Daddy!" This picture is the picture of a toddler trying his or her first steps. But we are God's toddlers. Let's bump in His knees continually. We will hear His voice guiding us.

Listen to the Preached Message

When you go to church or when you are in your car, listen to the preached message. God speaks to us through sermons. He speaks to us through testimonies also. Pay close attention to what people say in the pulpit. Even if you could preach better than that guy up there, please listen to the word. God chose them to preach today. Listen to them. I mean listen to God. You will be blessed abundantly.

Use Fleeces

God is not bothered by us. Our human civilities teach us to say, "I'm sorry to bother you, but...." God is not bothered at all. So, let's use the fleece if that is what will help us understand God's answer to our request. But beware of what James says. If we ask for something, we must believe that God will respond. We cannot use a fleece and doubt ourselves again. Either we use this fleece or use another sign, or we don't use a fleece at all. Let's not bear the blame of tempting God because we do not believe what our fleece reveals.

Watch the Signs

My dear friend, become good at reading the signs. Everything that exists in the physical world is the imperfect representation of what is in the invisible world. There are spiritual signposts that we do not see with a naked eye. But the eye of our soul will see these if we apply ourselves to learning the science of God. These invisible signs will show in our daily routine by the circumstances that God will create. God is the Master of the times and the circumstances. Pray that He will help you be alert and read the signs and circumstances that He will create to guide you.

Pay Attention to your Dreams

Pharaoh had a dream that repeated itself. Joseph interpreted it for him. His interpretation not only saved Egypt from a collapse, but it also saved surrounding nations and even the Nation of God: Israel. King Nebuchadnezzar had several dreams.

Daniel interpreted them all. They had predictions for the future.

Even, they prophesized about the coming of the Messiah. And when the Messiah was come and put to trial, Pilate's wife dreamed of the sanctity of Christ.

We believe all these accounts of pagan rulers. But we refute the idea that God can speak to us through our very dreams. That is not wise. God foretold the means of communication He will establish with us in the last days; we should not shun His voice this much anymore.

Listen to your Heart

Your heart is your transponder God put in you to communicate with you and you with Him. Listen to it. When nothing makes sense to you, check your heart. Something that is awkward to the brain might not be so awkward to your heart. The premise we need to get at is that you keep your heart with all diligence because if your heart is not clear with God, then it will deceive you. Clean your heart before God every morning and every night. Invite God in your heart always. He will connect with you and will not allow the fog of this world and the devil to cloud His communication with you.

Seek Advice

It is not always obvious to know the will of God. Since Adam and Eve sinned in the garden, the will of God has become a mystery for humankind. To follow it, we need to surround ourselves with the presence of God and the counsel of godly people.

Therefore, always have someone on call. What do I mean? Know someone in your circle of friends you can call for pruned and pure advice concerning the matters of faith.

Don't just hang out with superficial people. Know someone you trust who can be that person of sound spiritual advice. Consult with them when you want to hear God. Let me tell you: you must be that person for your friends too. As someone else polishes you, you as well must polish them.

Listen to the Audible Voice of God

If God spoke to Moses, Samuel, and Jesus, He can still speak with you audibly. God is not limited by space or time. If God chooses it, He will speak to you and you will literally hear His voice. Just be ready. Remember

that He has many channels through which He reaches us. None of those channels should be neglected. Let us expect to hear the voice of God before we depart from this world. If we prepare well, He will not allow anyone to trick us into hallucinations where we will think we heard the voice of God.

"The Lord bless you and keep you; The Lord make His face shine upon you, And be gracious to you; The Lord lift up His countenance upon you, And give you peace." In Jesus' name. Amen.

About the Author

Vitalis Essala helps individuals, groups, and organizations increase confidence in God, so that they can grow their influence and position themselves as leaders in their fields. The purpose he has in mind for this book is to help you know how to listen to God, so that you can establish a fruitful communication with The Almighty. Vitalis is a chaplain, preacher, life, spiritual, and leadership coach. He holds a Bachelor of Science in sociology and organizational leadership from Arizona State University and is pursuing his Master of Arts in religion at the Seventh-day Adventist Theological Seminary in Michigan, United States of America; he is a follower of Christ, a servant of the Lord, and a Bible student.

Other Products From This Author

Books

Act On Your Dream Today: The Principles of Stability and Human Excellence Part 1 – 2015

The Belief Vaccine: Identifying, Treating and Curing The Diseases of Self-Doubt – 2016

Mon Seul Péché (short novel in French) – 2017

5 Models of Prayer: How to Pray Fervently Well and Expose yourself to the Holy Spirit Constantly – 2018 (also in audio)

Audio CDs and Downloadables

Take a Sip: It's Self-confidence – 2018

How to listen to God (Audio)

The Bible Translated in Menguissa, a tribal language - shorturl.at/xERTY

Online Courses

Building Productivity: The Netflix Way (Udemy.com) – 2018 – serves students from 13 countries.

Practical guide for Cancer Survivors: Leading a Meaningful Life after Cancer (Teachable.com) – 2019

Winning Souls Ministries YouTube Channel -

Contact the Author

vitalisessala@gmail.com